607

C708 019 638 3

C000242192

SONG & DANCE

Edw 8.08		
12/08		
Forest Town		
Forest Town		
04/09		
RAVENSHEAD		
SELSTON		
- AUG 2009		
BALDERTON		
TEL. 707570		
12/09		

COUNTY LIBRARY

Please return / renew by the
last date shown.

ALSO BY JOHN FULLER

Fiction

Flying to Nowhere
The Adventures of Speedfall
Tell It Me Again
The Burning Boys
Look Twice
The Worm and the Star
A Skin Diary
The Memoirs of Laetitia Horsepole
Flawed Angel

Poetry

Fairground Music
The Tree That Walked
Cannibals and Missionaries
Epistles to Several Persons
The Mountain in the Sea
Lies and Secrets
The Illusionists
Waiting for the Music
The Beautiful Inventions
Selected Poems 1954 to 1982
Partingtime Hall (with James Fenton)
The Grey Among the Green
The Mechanical Body
Stones and Fires
Collected Poems
Now and for a Time
Ghosts
The Space of Joy

Criticism

The Sonnet
W.H. Auden: a Commentary

For Children

Herod Do Your Worst
Squeaking Crust
The Spider Monkey Uncle King
The Last Bid
The Extraordinary Wool Mill and Other Stories
Come Aboard and Sail Away

As Editor

The Chatto Book of Love Poetry
The Dramatic Works of John Gay
The Oxford Book of Sonnets
W.H. Auden: Poems Selected by John Fuller

SONG & DANCE

John Fuller

Chatto & Windus
LONDON

Published by Chatto & Windus 2008

9 8 7 6 5 4 3 2 1

Copyright © John Fuller 2008

John Fuller has asserted his right under the Copyright, Designs
and Patents Act 1988 to be identified as the author of this work

First published in Great Britain in 2008 by
Chatto & Windus
The Random House Group Ltd, 20 Vauxhall Bridge Road,
London SW1V 2SA

www.rbooks.co.uk

Addresses for companies within The Random House Group Limited
can be found at:
www.randomhouse.co.uk/offices.htm

The Random House Group Limited Reg. No. 954009

A CIP catalogue record for this book
is available from the British Library

ISBN 9 780 70118238 0

The Random House Group Limited makes every effort to ensure
that the papers used in its books are made from trees that have been
legally sourced from well-managed and credibly certified forests.
Our paper procurement policy can be found at:
www.rbooks.co.uk/environment

Typeset by Palimpsest Book Production Ltd, Grangemouth, Stirlingshire

Printed and bound in the UK by
CPI Mackays, Chatham ME5 8TD

CONTENTS

Nottinghamshire County Council

Community Services

Askews	
821.914 FUL	£9.00

SONG

FLORIO DRINKING SONG

Packington's Pound

All you lovers of claret get ready to swallow,
With gullet distended and cheek-pouches hollow.
The bottle has shoulders for shrugging off dregs
And the claret comes running on little red legs.
     Now if Nick needs a screw
     He'll know what to do
     As long as the angle of entry is true.
So the neck of the bottle is eased of its bung
And the wine like a waterfall washes the tongue.

Now Richard is ready for mosel and hock,
Debbie's nostrils dilate and her taste-buds unlock.
They are close to their bliss, just the bottle between
(The hock is in yellow, the mosel in green).
     Now Elise like a lamb
     Or a perfect madame
     Pours an inch for herself and a saucer for Sam,
While the rest root about for a cork they can chew
And the wine like a window enhances the view.

It's a race to get whiffled, forgetting the food.
If the Blue Nun is chilly, then rip off her snood!
John lurches to broach her but sprawls on the table,
Leaving Peter the cork and poor Robert the label.
     Now Bernard's in front
     As he pulls off a stunt
     With his palm on her neck and his thumb in her
        punt.
Oh what a rare flavour, oh what a grand shape!
And the wine like a widow remembers the grape.

Michèle is judicious and rolls the white nectar
Round her mouth as Achilles round Troy dragged dead
    Hector,
And she purses her lips with a sensuous care

That reminds us (though faintly) of kissing or prayer.
> Now Simon and Mark
> Are as damp as the Ark
> (And the latter will have to be up with the lark)
With the bottle bequeathing its dreams to the heart
And the wine like a watch saying 'Time to depart'.

But the drinkers remember, before the night ends,
Peculiar, potent and absent old friends:
Raskolnikov Oliver, Dorrit Louise,
Alison's haircut and Fanny's bare knees.
> Oh woe, now that Nicky's
> Not here to drink wickies.
> Where's Frank and his ciggies? (and God knows where
> Mick is).
All the past is fast fading and fruitlessly beckoning
And the wine like a waiter insists on the reckoning.

So here's to the Florio figures of yore
Who wave to us now from the opposite shore:
Clare out in Cowley and Julie in Leamington
Pounding away on her scabrous old Remington,
> Nenna the talk
> Of most of New York,
> And Lucy in Paris awaiting the stork,
We think of them fondly. Oh would they were here!
Still the wine, like a wishbone, can make them seem near.

NEVER KNEW

A Song for Fernandel

When I first grew up they told me
'Don't just hold me:
You must enfold me!
Listen to the beating of your heart!
And take a grip. And make a start.'
But I was not enthusiastic,
Not as elastic,
Not so gymnastic
That I could shoot Love's feathered dart.
I'd rather read. Or eat fruit tart.
      Never knew
Is like sitting out a dance
      Never knew
Is what they say of maiden aunts.
Why are they lonely on their own?
Is it that that makes them blue?
Or is it that they never knew?

Life has many compensations
If you have patience
With your relations
When they sidle up to say
'It's surely time you named the day?'
If they come insinuating
That you are waiting
Too long for mating,
All you need to do is smile
And sing this little song with style:
      Never knew
Well, it's better the devil you know
      Never knew
Means taking it nice and slow.
What's the thing that people cry for?
What is it makes them blue?
Aren't I glad I never knew!

Yet ignorance can be injurious.
Sometimes I'm curious
Or simply furious.
A perfect Jeeves among the smutty maids,
I never even saw the Ace of Spades!
It's at the least unenterprising.
It's not surprising
It's tantalising.
Life is something like a motorcade,
And though my looks will never fade
      Never knew
Is an epitaph I'll hate
      Never knew
Is almost worse than being too late.
The peculiar thing that people crave,
That thrills them through and through,
They'll have to say I never knew.

THE CURSE OF THE GLASS BACK LANKY COOLIE

It were clear pop to the terminal
And feathers all the way,
But since that I've been pounded
I've nowt but this to say:

Does he think I don't care?
Does he think I'll take it lying
Down? Or burst out crying?
Dark time, it's unfair.

He's borrowed me dear dolly.
He's borrowed me rough-and-tumble.
It's more than a bit of a grumble
At a smite of lemonjolly.

It's the end of all living.
It's the end of all joy.
He's borrowed me goosey toy
And it's past believing.

He's a driver on the Blue Streak,
Down the Bowling Green,
So fast he can't be seen
From Friday to next week.

Ay, but I've words in me pay.
I know a charm to say,
And the words'll have their way
And I will have me day.

It were clear pop to the terminal
And feathers all the way,
But since that I've been pounded
I've nowt but this to say:

Give me the right deep breath
Of the bandsman who breathes as he plays
So I can curse for days
While planning his lingering death.

I want him wet with fear.
I want him wet and dirty.
I'll slowly count to thirty
And make him disappear.

He rides tight as a button
But I can see right through him.
I'll take him and undo him.
I'll split him up like mutton.

I'll split him up like long tom.
I'll see his nozzle break
Like navvies' wedding cake.
And send him where he come from.

It were clear pop to the terminal
And feathers all the way,
But since that I've been pounded
I've nowt but this to say:

I'll poke him in his fireplaces.
They'll call him tunnel mouth,
I'll do it, it's the truth.
I want to smash both his faces.

I want to lay bare his bone
In all the tenderest parts.
I want to hear his goshy farts.
Give me a heart of stone.

Give me the grip of gorilla.
Give me the pitiless gaze
Of a man with fingers and ways
That have long been those of a killer.

Give me the strength of jar-tops,
And the eye of jumping jacks.
I want him to stop in his tracks.
I want him to fall where he stops.

It were clear pop to the terminal
And feathers all the way,
But since that I've been pounded
I've nowt but this to say:

I lay out this curse like a plan.
The jewels are marked with a cross.
And I'll squeeze him until the loss
Makes him no more a man.

Ay, and I'll take his wee snap-scran,
And squeeze out all the sauce,
And squeeze and squeeze until the loss
Makes him no more a man.

SONG OF ABSENCE

The space that was filled with the ash tree
Is displaying a desolate blue,
That lack is a path in the bracken
Which led to the ridge with a view,
That gap was a gate that we fastened
To stop ewes and lambs getting through,
And the grass is knee-high in the garden
And the scythe makes a rust of the dew.

The creaking that comes from the stairwell
At the silent tread of a shoe,
The warmth and the crease in a cushion,
The flower in the vase that looks new,
The creosote smell on the gatepost,
The trickling sound from the loo,
The knock on the door that is no one,
The absence upstairs that is you.

The morning has lost its momentum,
The afternoon's nothing to do,
The evening's completely self-centred
And all its assumptions untrue,
But worst is the stillness of night-time,
For ever a quarter-past two
When dwelling on shapes in the darkness
Is no nearer to sleeping, or you.

THE ONLY GOT SO MUCH BLUES

You gave me plenty, but I want more of it.
    Love is too good to waste.
Twice is exciting, but I need three or four of it.
    It's a problem that's got to be faced.
        Avarice? Not nice.
        They say it's a vice.
        I'll take it,
        But I don't make it.
        You were high-minded
        And I ignored it.
        What you need, I can't find it.
        I can't afford it!
I've only got so much and I want much more.

Spendaholics make a mess of it.
    There's everything to lose.
The more you want, I'll end up with less of it:
    I'll have to refuse.
        Hands on my neck?
        What the heck!
        Lips at my ear:
        Do I care?
        You make your claim, dear,
        And I applaud it.
        It's such a shame, dear,
        That I can't afford it.
I've only got so much and I want much more.

We take the smooth and we take the rough of it.
　　　　Any romance is flawed.
But once we get it, we can't get enough of it.
　　　　It's pretty mean to hoard.
　　　　　　　Trout are ticklish,
　　　　　　　Pickles are picklish.
　　　　　　　You say you're hot
　　　　　　　And that I'm not.
　　　　　　　You want your prize, dear,
　　　　　　　And me to award it.
　　　　　　　I'll summarise, dear:
　　　　　　　I can't afford it!
I've only got so much and I want much more.

TWO SECULAR HYMNS

1 Rights

The right to step on the ladder
If we can foot the cost,
The right to persuade by letter
If our heading is embossed,
The right to cheer our leader
When the Rubicon's been crossed,
The right to care for the loser,
The right to despise the lost.

The right to join the powerful,
The right to persevere,
The right to adjust our vowels
In the effort to sound sincere,
The right to love our neighbour
As a means of disguising fear,
The right to provide for our children
In the next financial year.

The right to manage the market,
The right to weather the storm,
The right to buy all the blankets
To be sure of keeping warm,
The right to define the abnormal
In the interests of the norm,
The right to a full confession
From those who won't conform.

The right to claim our expenses
If the carriages are crammed,
The right to lead in the champion
When the stable door has slammed,
The right to tune our conscience
When every signal's jammed
And the silence of the wretched
Drowns the drivel of the damned.

Though every book be unmade
When nations make their dash
From the last available shade
And death with its vain panache
Salutes at the last parade,
Though all that is written may fade
And the language fall to ash,
We need not be dismayed.

For all of us have preferred
To think experience real,
And wouldn't it be absurd
To think that words can heal
What has or hasn't occurred?
We write what we've seen and heard,
Write what we know and feel
And make the moment a word.

The feelings travel fast
And writing asks this rule:
Each single day is vast
And has a powerful pull
Which words should try to blast
In shapes from the quarried past.
When books and hearts are full,
Only the feelings last.

HOW FAR?

How far is it to Carcassonne?
I'll stir the dust until
I reach that glittering place I crave,
Heat-haunted citadel.

You were away before us,
With something on your mind,
Reckless of all horizon
And all you left behind.

Your friends of the cold morning,
The friends you lived among,
Who worked with you, and fished with you
They heard you sing this song:

'How far is it to Carcassonne?
How difficult to find?
The years run on and on and on
Like waves upon the mind.'

How far is it to Carcassonne?
We sat at night alone.
I knew my heart was full enough.
The sea and shore were one.

You looked away. I heard you say:
'I'm going to Carcassonne.
My weary feet are stoutly shod,
My shoes are full of blood and bone
And while I have my breath, by God,
I'll go to Carcassonne.'

How far is it to Carcassonne?
How difficult to find?
The years run on and on and on
And I am left behind.

Although I do not see an end,
I do not have the patience left
To face blank stares with smiles,
For I shall soon be gone.

The skies are rent, the rock is cleft,
And we shall soon be dead.
How far is it to Carcassonne?
How far is it, how far?

How far is it to Carcassonne?
No trace of you is there,
Nor anywhere upon this road I tread,
Nor anywhere, nor anywhere.

RASCASSE

A shoal like a Calder mobile appears
Posing with parallel fins,
Little blue fishes with tails like shears
And well-tuned fears that are better than ears
For sharks with their chinless grins.

And in between the two extremes
Of fry in a state of fright
And the cruising drama of their dreams,
Between the teeth and the prey that teems,
The flight and the terrible bite

Comes a moment of fun, as one by one
There enter the pink rascasse
Wearing a curious look, like a nun
Remembering something private she's done
Halfway through the Mass.

You've seen it in court on the face of Charles Laughton,
That Black Cap, bad-smell leer:
A touch of class like a '99 Corton
Suppressing a snigger like the plays of Joe Orton
Or the mad disgust of *Lear*.

On a fish of a certain size, you know,
Self-righteousness sits oddly,
But the surliness is only for show:
Their thoughts as they twiddle to and fro
Are plaintive and ungodly.

(The sea's an old bowl of soup, my dears,
And we are the tipsy frosh.
It's been about for a billion years
And it's salty like the sting in tears
That doesn't come out in the wash.

A crusty fish, a whiskered fish,
Must never, but never, lose face.
The song expresses our fervent wish
Not to end up in a steaming dish
With the rest of the bouillabaisse.)

'The hand that placed the planets loosed the thunder.
The hand that piped the blood betrayed a blunder.
The hand that made the blunder sent a flood.
The hand that formed the flounder gave it mud.
      Rascasse! Rascasse!
      A rose sedan! A mailed cuirass!
      Marine retread of Zinedine Zidane!
      Late call? Doubtful ball!
Anything's better than ending up dead.

The hand that fingered Adam was the same.
The hand that bluffed the baize gave up the game.
The hand that raised the city made a bid.
The hand that stirred the squirlu squashed the squid.
      Rascasse! Rascasse!
      Enversez-moi une demi-tasse!
      Just like I said (mwah! mwah!)
      Vents violents? Soyez prudents!
Anything's better than ending up dead.

The hand that rocked the cradle rocked the rocks.
The hand that signed the paper felled the ox.
The hand that calmed the waters lit the hob.
The hand that made the soup turned up the knob.
      Rascasse! Rascasse!
      Godfrey Daniel! Godfrey Cass!
      King Charles's head! King Charles's spaniel!
      Rouille? Phooey!
Anything's better than ending up dead.'

&

MY LIFE ON THE MARGINS OF CELEBRITY

I sat on Beatrix Lehmann's knee, terrified that she was
    undead;

I saw Laurel and Hardy alive at the Lewisham Hippodrome,
    and they were gratified by my laughter;

I bowed to Queen Mary, widow of George V, in Greenwich
    Park, and from her limousine of midnight hue she
    nodded graciously back;

I was inspected in full uniform by Field-Marshal Montgomery:
    his cornflower-blue eyes passed within twenty inches
    of mine, and he departed in a bullet-proof car;

I sang for Vaughan Williams, his great head sunk on his
    waistcoat, neither awake nor asleep;

I watched Jonathan Miller lift a white mouse by its tail and
    drop it in a killing-bottle for me as an illustration of
    something or other;

I saw Frank Swift pick up a football with one hand;

I waited in the wings for my own entrance while Oliver
    Sacks played de Falla's 'Ritual Fire Dance' in a sash
    and a lurid spotlight;

I asked T. S. Eliot what he was writing, and his answer shall
    remain a secret;

I rang up the curtain on Dennis Potter in his first public
    performance, playing the part of a Romanian-French
    playwright;

I trod the throbbing boards of an ocean liner with Burt
    Lancaster, who was very small, and who smiled his
    characteristically delicate sneering smile;

I was asked to stay on in my first job, but politely declined
    and was succeeded in office by the Earl of Gowrie;

I drove Edward Albee to Niagara Falls, where he was silent
among the thickly-iced trees;

I held Sam Mendes in my arms, but was more interested in
his father's collection of Japanese pornography;

I brushed away cobwebs that had been sprayed on my hair
by David Attenborough;

I played heads-bodies-and-legs with Henry Moore;

The Poet Laureate sent me reams of his verse, which I
regretfully refused to publish;

I handed Debra Winger a glass of wine and did not tell her
who I was;

I played against William Golding's French Defence and
infiltrated my King's Knight to d6 and he couldn't
avoid going a piece down;

And all this is true, and life is but a trail of dust between the
stars;

The unremembered shall be forgotten, and the remembered
also;

The dead shall be dead, and also the living.

from THE SPELLCHECKER'S GUIDE TO POETRY

Of the very beginnings there is not much to be said,
Since many readers find ancient poetry as dead as dead.
You will come across Longhand and the Poet of *Join*
Where there is much to concern both spirit and groin.
One who is a good deal livelier and franker
Than you'd expect is good old Geoffrey Chancre.
His *Trolls and Crusade* is a work that ought to be read.
After him, there is Unbar who liked to flyte,
But not much else until Skeleton and Wight.

The Elizabethans come next, but many are wary
Of Sponsor and his excursions into Faery:
There seems to be something protracted about his material,
Involving the lengthy quests of Guyana and Arterial.
Students nowadays prefer plays with enormous casts
Like Marline's spectacular *Doctor Fasts*
Where a don turns into a voluptuary,
Or the one where the King fatally takes a shine
To Gravestone, or we see the ridiculous ambition of
    Timberline.

But beautifully best and impossible to disregard
Are the great involving plays by our national Bard:
We love it when the lovers become entangled
Or when King Ear enters with Curdle strangled,
When Gestured takes poison by mistake, when Other
Is deceived by the evil Ago and is eager to smother
His innocent wife, when Shellac's bond is marred,
When Flats boasts to the Prince after their escapade,
When Lentos threatens Politeness, or Cabin, Marinade.

AT A DISTANCE

*'We owe to the Middle Ages the two worst inventions of humanity
– gunpowder, and romantic love.'* André Maurois

Cannon still cold when talky Troy was sacked,
Hacking of kneecaps was an intimate act
Promptly performed, risked for a clear reward:
City or woman taken with the sword.
Or death with honour (Old High Hildebrand,
Prut in pure, fighting hand to hand).

The last ditch, where the hero slaked his thirst,
Was simply a drier version of the first,
Fate wrote his destiny in lines of blood
That went on beating, even in the mud.
The single killer faced somebody's brother
And Mother Earth was just another mother.

Heroic couples met on field or bed,
For some few seconds, or for ever, dead.
Heroic couplets symbolise their pairing:
Combative, driven, sparring, feinting, sharing.
Alike in love or war, their bodies met,
Weapons between, in eager tête-à-tête.

Consider now the heirs of Christendom:
Manic idealists blown to kingdom come,
The mercenary marching on his belly,
Bertrans de Born, Dante and Percy Shelley,
The liberal opinions of the highbrow,
Flat Nagasaki, lines to a lady's eyebrow.

Once God was animated by our fears;
Nothing today excites us like ideas.
Once we heard clearly what our murderer yelled.
No strong views now: 'extreme views, weakly held'.
Our adorations hopelessly explode,
And war is a dramatic episode.

Couplets were shelved with a Romantic curse
In favour of blank, free, Projective verse.
Our longings have been blank and free too long,
And couples too contented with a song.
Now mind works at a distance, calculating,
And all perfection's waiting, waiting, waiting.

Hard to distinguish epicure and glutton:
The feminist is fingering her button,
Battle-lines are thrown up on a screen
And tired professors tell us what they mean.
In love and war, strong magic plays its part:
Semtex, a gatefold stapled through her heart.

FEAR OF NAMING

Not animal, not bird
Is the occluded word,
Nor fish nor insect make
Your shuddering shoulders shake
(Ugh! A writhing necklace!).
It is finless and legless.
Rustling in the brake,
It makes the heather quake,
A thing that irks and rankles,
A thing that with bare ankles
You suddenly tread awake
(A twig that doesn't break).
Crossing a trickling creek is
To wish for boots not sneakers:
It bites, for goodness' sake.
Your foot's not fillet steak.
When Romans once turned scabious,
Lo! there was Esculapius
As one: 'I undertake
To cure: a piece of cake!'
At Lawrence's water-trough
(Until he chased it off)
It came one noon to slake
Its thirst. You know it spake
In sly Miltonic accents
To Eve. The Anglo-Saxons
Called it a wyrm (their drakes
Could fly, and so could Blake's).
The Ancient Mariner watched it.
The Macbeths only scotched it.
Was Lamia a fake?
A Lady of the Lake?
The flickering of that tongue!
The glittering eye among
Its folds, the scales opaque
And jewelled like a sheik!

That litheness of the lynx,
That sphincter in the sphinx
In curves that make you ache!
There must be some mistake:
Her lure was real to Keats
Whose mind between the sheets
Played for a higher stake
Than I could, give or take
Another rhyme, a riddle
That seems to be all middle,
No ending. For God's sake,
Do I dream or wake?
Which is the dance? The dancer?
Give me, please, the answer.

A CRITIC

Gup, lass!
Front of the class,
Quick now, come out fighting!
Did you find it exciting,
This daubed paper,
This clogged boot-scraper,
Glib as a label,
Garbled as Babel?
What does print confer
On such hauteur?
It leaves you where you were,
That's what,
Like as not
In ignorance
That you're a dunce.
So you took your guesses
For successes?
Self-righteousness's
Sneaky anatomy lessons?
PC's quintessence?
PC on the take,
Ms Mistake!
What on earth went wrong?
You opened your lips too long,
A sermon at Evensong.
Hardly surprising
That you're the Cat of Categorising,
The Sister of systematising,
The Or of theorising,
The Mother Dog of Dogmatising.
Away with you, enemy of art!
Self-important person, depart!
You are a continuing false start.
Towards you the starter's gun
Will turn from the sun.
Now you must really run!

Run if you like, but we shall catch you.
Run like a watery colic, like a tinker's snatch, you
Will never get away.
We will take you to the cleaners
For your misdemeanours.
You are the piss in the *pis aller*,
Your briefs are marbled with café-au-lait,
Your conversation has the rare bouquet
Of the absolutely unendurable,
Your slightest faux-pas's uninsurable.
Think you are welcome
Because you talcum
Your picnic eggs
And wax your legs?
Because you can smile and frown at once?
Your vehemence
Empties a conference.
You are too Concerned.
You never learned
That common sense
Is otherwise
Than knowing surmise.
That smear of innocence
Widening your eyes
Simply signifies
The cobra's sway before it strikes.
Your glower is the glower of shrikes.
You and Bill Sikes are lookalikes.
All that you dream of sex
Was learned in bibliothèques
And what you want of men is merely thuggish,
Borrowing Caligula's vain wish
For Roman necks.
God, what did your father do?
What did he do to you
That makes you seethe,
That makes you sorry that men breathe?
Did he make you wear white socklets?

29

Did he take away your chocolates?
There, there then: did never kind hand
Descend on you unplanned,
Friendly and taken so?
And made you glow?
And did you never fall?
A finger on your small
Morsel of the future find
You not entirely disinclined?
Perhaps you never had the chance.
You never were the dance
Nor yet the dancer,
And gave no happy answer.
Though they showed you the tune,
Though you howled on the dune
Like Bodyform, your brain leaked blue
Through knowing what to do.
Now it is like the chestnut,
Floury and dry, isn't it?
Why so eager,
Your gift being so meagre?
Well, well, we shall see.
Remember, if you want to be
A missionary with a mission,
To assume the right position.
That the highest of high-flyers
Are Cretan philosophers, that liars
Are often cannibals, every Cretan
A liar – and missionaries get eaten.

VARIATION ON SHAPCOTT

When the Old Man suddenly rubbed me awake
I was already aroused, yawning and reaching upwards,
Skinny as a rib, just a slip of a something
With a taut belly and extremely long legs.
I knew immediately what I was intended for,
Dropped like a hairy yet naked egg
Into such a heavily populated garden.
But that gracile creature with his delicate yard
Lolling like a pink comma across his leg
Was not the greatest thing I was up against.
When the Old Man nudged me into his arms
I could only think: nothing will come of nothing
With all that other wild howling pulling me downwards,
Proboscis, slung bull, ape-gland, snake.

TOWER

This clock is hand- and faceless. Look: and you look
In vain for a gold disc. Or numbers which
Are the wild trysts in your appointment book.
Only the ear knows its deceitful pitch
And aches to hear those stone reverberations,
The cadences that limit and exhort us,
Dividing duty into lamentations
And plodding hours into distinguished quarters.

Listen: beyond the tower rise larks and linnets
In antiphons of timeless amorous rhyme.
But we must live the striking day within its
Heartless mocking of such paradigm,
Another clapped-out rugby-side of minutes
Sent shambling from the muddied field of time.

QUICKER BY THE KLEINE

At Grindelwald one Frederick Fletcher
Desired me to inscribe his *Manfred*.
He cried: 'My Lord, I shall be candid.
A grocer cannot understand it.'
I stuck my stock into the gletscher
And told him kindly: 'No one *can*, Fred.
You have to read it with persistence.
Ideally you should read left-handed,
And when you feel you're *in der Quetsche*
Look to your sister for assistance.'

Under the duvet Nanny's calling,
Promising a sticky kiss;
The Lorelei is crooning in
Her bottomless crevasse of bliss;
Here on the Jungfrau snow is falling
With a delicious sense of sin.
Manfred drives a grocer frantic
Insisting that he's not romantic
(Romanticism is enthralling;
A grocer's everything that's Swiss).

Hell is the grandest of hotels.
Hell is *gemütlich* and quite roomy
(I have one foot already there).
I make a thing of being gloomy
But don't particularly care.
Drown me in the Dardanelles!
Hang me, and so despatch me neck first!
Blacken my actions in the *Chronicle*!
I'll simply smile, adjust my monocle
And mock the headline over breakfast.

I limp the high exclusive line
Which cannot take account of grocers
Even my breakfast is a grossness
That I can scarce acknowledge mine.
I am ascetic in moroseness:
I actually enjoy the guilt
Poetically, without neurosis.
It's just the way my psyche's built.
It's like the bubbles in my wine.
It's like the swagger in my kilt.

Let grocers cross the Grosse Scheidegg!
I shall do something altogether
More appropriate to the weather
And modulate into the minor.
Sing me to sleep beneath the eaves!
Spring will come, with fresher leaves
(Spoonfuls of leaves, in fact, a quarter
Of lemon and some boiling water).
I'll break my fast on tea not fried egg
And get there quicker by the Kleine.

Among the Victorians particularly worthy of mention,
Is the lachrymose Laureate, Alfred, Lord Tension,
Author of 'Epoch Ardent', 'Oneness', 'Mud',
And 'Garret and Lighten' in which there is lots of blood.
Influenced by the Romantics in his youth,
Like Kits he was a seeker after Beauty rather than Truth
And yet of nameless truths he had a fine apprehension.
He neglected his appearance, and became especially forlorn
When he heard of the death of freedom-loving Lord Bighorn.

He used to dash out into the night to seek attention
By repeating his name till he fainted: 'Tension, Tension,
Tension, Tension, Tension, Tension, Tension, Tension.
Tension, Tension, Tension, Tension, Tension, Tension,
Tension, Tension, Tension, Tension, Tension, Tension . . .'
At Cambridge he embraced several young men who
Regarded his affection with the utmost incomprehension
And were cleverer than him, like Gallstone and Arthur Halloo.
When Halloo died, Tension made an extraordinary hullabaloo.

A DOZEN VICTORIAN AUTOGRAMS

1

A tale of tenderness and a sealed fate,
A tale as fatal as a frosted leaf,
Fears, early fears, a lad feared lost at sea,
Years, endless years, on a deserted reef,
Tears, salty tears, and no dry eyes we see,
A seafarer forlorn, released too late.

Too early fastened to a tenant lease!
None dare to read a tale so really sad,
For Arden's sorry story tells one only
Of stolen years and of a loyal lad
Safe at last – yet altered, lonely.
Don't rely on art to send release.

2

We were not begging to be torn
Into being, not begging to be born.
We were bent on getting to t'Tower
(Not being inert, nor in error;
Not grown worn, nor gibbering in terror).
Entering on bitter winter now:
To win or not to win?
'Twere better not to be born, I trow.

3

No rebel memory mine.
Nobly, I'll remember.
I'll tremble, limb by limb,
My one and only moor!
No Byron in one lonely tomb,
Bone by bone, ember by terrible ember.
Yet . . . mile on mile, O my moor!

4

Hail, ami!
Wilt halt? Wilt wait?
What am I? An animal in a hat? Naw.
(Am I a Milan wit? A Taiwan tin-man? *Naw*!)

O I am atman, I am *alma* in Latin, I am all anima.
I tilt at Law at whim. I am *anti*-Law.

I am thin. I am tan. I am anal.
I am a man with a man mania.

5

How dear to me, that late maternal tear!
Her olden world, how dear! The wet mer-town
That mother made me want, how real and new!
And when the Roman led hard Dante down,
To what warm torment? And to what hatred, Lear?

Men who knew wrath, and knew an elder Law.
No hero now doth wear a noted helm,
No herald wreath that the old era wore.
Ah, now the loathèd modern world doth whelm
The heart to death! We hear that tear no more.

We are the Dane who hate to hold a throne.
We learn the modern method, ream on ream.
Lead me to Etna now! And let the Rhône
Wend on and on. No wonder that we dream.
We are not worth The Word. We are alone.

6

Instant historian, O antic heart!
Inter in roses these so trenchant tears
That reach, in their researches, into art!
The ear resists the stricter tones it hears:
The Antichrist, his hair, his scars, his horns;
Sistine chants in ancient iciness;
Instant crosses; Easters rich in thorns;
Resistance, contests, strain, anarchic stress.

Sister in Christ, chosen, I reach to thee!
The choir eternal carries thee to a star.
The thresher's risen hair is thine, she sees
The artist stitch his instant rosaries.
She is a sacristan, as Christians are
That race their chariots to the archaic Tree.

7

Lammas-morrow, arrows will assail
Armorial walls, O swallow!
Sir Silas will swill,
Sir Silas will wallow.
Maria will wail, as a lass will.
War allows a moral,
O swallow, swallow:
'As arms roam warm,
So Law's a mirror.'
All is worms, alas.
All is sorrow.

8

Shy as a dryad, dost say?
Or a rash moth? Or a mardy stray?
A mad tryst, so thy drama starts,
Thy arms a host to amatory darts.
Too moody to tarry,
A hasty dash to marry —
So hast trod today a road most hard:
Hoary moor to mossy marsh to dry oast-yard,
A martyr to thy sorry story,
A myth, a moth to a sad star.

9

High in my dreamy parish, dragon-skied,
Many-a-morning's skeined on a leaning slope
And laid, as shining as names are (spare, odd, pied),
Like many-garlanded men in manly hope,
Marked as holy (e'en on a dandled edge, a
Sheer air-ladder) in God's ample ledger.

Mornings are all spark and prayer: only
Men die in sheer plod and ashen skin,
Like any dismayed philosopher, as lonely
As aspens, rank on rank, all pining in
A damaged landskip, learning God's hidden grammar.
Ask, and ye shall dread His handled hammer!

10

Was I a radical, a class warrior?
I dared our social code.
(Words are easier, words were all I owed.)
We are all older, rosier, wider — sorrier.

I was called coward, ere law did
    Worse deeds;
I was ill-rewarded
    As are all rare creeds;
I was called lewd (I ordered a lad
    As we do a car).
Desire is sacred, dew-clad
    As roses are,
Carried across a wall.

Desire is a wild card, desire is a cold idol
(Dear boy, I swear I drew a rare ace!)
Desire is order erased, desire is a riddle.
I wore desire as ladies wear classic lace.
Desire is Ariel's role, desire is droll,
Desire is a crocodile's face, desire is a doll.
(Dear boy, as I was called a liar,
I swear desire is a discarded law-case.)

11

Seu mens sana, seu Moses musa mea

Hush! Shame has no human name
Nausea has no human uses.
    Ashen senses,
    Ashen hues.
Muses seem nonsense. No man amuses.

12

Angry, Danny? In a paddy?
Unruly during a daring run?
A drag, drill? Gun-drill, laddy?
All day guarding a dark grey gun?

All in, Danny? Kipping all day?
Appalling liar in a darn gun-yard,
All day, any day, undying day,
Drunk, and all in, playing guard.

Drink up, Danny, draining a pink,
Arguing in Urdu, gulping a gin,
In daily ruin, pally in drink,
A grand, plug-ugly, bragging grin!

Play up, Danny, play up, lad!
King and killing, praying and lying
Pulling rank in dirk and plaid,
And gradually dying.

THE POET ORDERS HIS MARRIAGE AT
ST MARYLEBONE CHURCH

RB and EBMB, 12 September 1846

1

In and out I weave
Like a double double u
And the pillars patient as spindles receive the waiting skein.
In and out, and back
And forth, I await my cue
Where Hardwick's Corinthian nods to Nash's *mise-en-scène*.

2

Outside, the daily hubbub,
The ordinary rush
Of flies, with the spin and bounce of their wheels as they speed
    to the city.
Inside, the timeless silence,
A whiff of the old God-hush
That induces a wonder at infinite pain and infinite pity.

3

Six pillars, six
Minutes (I counted them off)
That it takes at her pace of quavers to get to the steps of the church:
From her father's ignorance
To the beadle's inquisitive cough
Full six unending minutes, I found in my fond research.

4

With the licence in my pocket
I made my own rehearsal,
Counted the steps and minutes that will seal the loving decision
Which now is set on its course,
Running without reversal
To the full and final chords of its grand initial vision.

5

With the licence in my pocket
And my inmost self professing
A ready trust in the service of the heart to be born afresh,
    I demanded the plainest rites:
    The text that defines God's blessing,
The touch of his finger that feels for the soul and makes one flesh.

6

The sexton under the tower
With his ready foot in a stirrup
Offered to tread the bells, but I said I would have no bells.
    The organ's *unda maris*
    Was oozing out like syrup,
But I forbade it: nothing but Goldhawk's book of spells.

7

Now six minutes since
She left her house for me
And here I wait with my loving cousin declaring his fitness
    To sign me over to life
    And love eternal, and she
With a steady tread to meet me here, and her maid as witness.

8

We are love's actors, we
Are waiting in our wings,
Watched by the critical world and gilded angels' faces
    Smudged with the smoke of theatre,
    Where the psalmist surely sings
That our lines are fallen unto us in pleasant places.

9

She who has been invited
Will shortly be in sight,
And the tide is running like dreams before the light of the morning
    The blood says, This is your chance
    To get there by candlelight,
And life draws its bearded and dripping anchor without warning.

10

Unload me at hot Cythera
With the harbourmaster's winch
And let my barrels be broached by love inspecting her borders!
Uncork my animal spirits
And pour out half an inch
And let the attentive future stand by awaiting my orders!

11

What shall they be? To be drained
To the last drop, to aspire?
Or to add one thing to another, the daily considered choice?
To lie in the swoon of the spirit
Or to spark and to take fire
Till the body survives its sentence and becomes a sounding voice?

12

Our wish, as we know, is both
The sum of its small attentions
And the large idea which has no distinct embodiment,
Until we suddenly find it
Declaring its intentions
And making its claim upon us, as being what we meant.

13

And so by indirection
We move towards a goal
That is always revealed to us in stages, like a play:
We try to learn our parts
And the parts are parts of a whole
That we must write ourselves, yet act out straight away.

14

The future bows politely:
It will surely do our will
As much as time can spare and decency allows,
And though it disapprove
It takes its wages still
And looks on silently with amused and lifted brows.

15

As for the sullen past,
It is left with nothing to do
But to squirrel away its secrets under rusty locks
Or feign forgetfulness
Or suddenly turn on you
And become your guilty familiar, an insistent chatterbox.

16

Only the moment is pure
Of connivance and accusation.
Only the moment itself is free of the hope or regret
That soon enough crowds upon
Our glad improvisation.
Only the moment has not yet learned to fear or forget.

17

Now it is time to act
As the four of us meet together,
And little is said as hands touch, heads incline and smile
In rueful acknowledgement that
It is insignificant whether
We walk in inappropriate pairs or in bridal style.

18

But like a dawn duel,
Each plighted and their second
Enters bravely through the mists of their unwished furtiveness.
None to give, or be given?
No one till now has reckoned
On the power of old tradition over bold assertiveness.

19

For a faint failing of form
Haunts the thing we want
To proceed without procedure (as though such a thing could be),
Makes us wince at the beadle's collar,
The verger's hat in the font,
The uncleared coils of rope, and such incongruity.

20

And now, as the words are recited
And we suddenly reach the most
Significant part of the play, the ring in the hot clasped glove,
There is a ghost here.
It is your father's ghost,
The living, the absent, the terrible — terrible in his love.

21

He stands where he ought to stand,
Unseen, unknowing, unknown,
And I feel him growing there like a frigid chill in the blood,
Like Acrisius in his tower,
Like Mozart's statue of stone,
Like the dragon defending the apples of gold, like a worm in the
bud.

22

And his ghost eyes the yellow ring
Placed on the leather book,
The blind-tooled commonplace blue of a Book of Common
Prayer,
As the curate takes it up
With hardly so much as a look
And gives it back to me for you and your finger to wear.

23

And just for a moment I quail
Before the invisible glare
That lingers with disbelief, and will continue to linger
Upon that empty shape
Resting on God's word there,
Heavy with our intent, now full upon your finger.

24

But dearest, our ghosts we defy:
In a moment the thing is done,
As a boat whose pilot sees her out through the widening estuary
Is at once in the open sea,
And we together are one
With the strangely familiar shape of our names in the dust of
the vestry.

25

You pause as if in a dream
And are given a glass of water,
And you start again in these first few minutes of married life
To sign, in unbelief
That you are still a daughter
(Or so you must name yourself) before you may be a wife.

26

And the talkative, puzzled verger,
Happy to take my gold,
Attempts on the steps to assert the sanctity of marriage
To a couple apparently reckless,
Though clearly disturbingly old,
Who leave him in rapt mid-sentence, each to their separate carriage.

27

And those six pillars support
A triumphant cupola
As a working week lays abundant groundwork for our devotion,
And high above our journey
There shines a single star
Compelling our hearts like keels to the receiving ocean.

28

The church itself is unchanged,
Yet silently proclaims
From its hallowed space, as it reaches aloft from London's grime,
That here have been safely lodged
An eager pair of names
That will lie in the annals of the parish, and of time.

THE TRANS-SEXUAL CIRCUS

Androgynist acrobats archly air
Body-bulging balloon-filled bosoms! Bare
Cossack-riding columbines! Cross-dressed clowns!
Delightfully developed drag-queen drowns!
Extravagant elephants erect ears!
Falstaffian fan-dancer's furtive fears!
Gender-defined Grimaldi: golly gee!
Hermaphrodite Houdini! Half-male, he!
In-betweeners, intending inverts ill!
Jam-rag-juggling Jeremy! Jockstrapped Jill!
Knickerbockered knife-thrower's kinky knee!
Lion-tamers' lace-ruffled Levis, Lee?
Man-womanly magician's mouish mood!
Never-never neurotics, nearly nude!
Organ-transplant odalisques open out
Punch-is-Judy's pyjamas' phallic pout!
Quasimodo's quick-firing questions: 'Queer?'
'Revisionist?' Rope-walker's raunchy rear!
Solitary stilt-walkers sadly strip!
Trampolining transvestites' turned-on trip!
Unusually upsetting urnings use
Velcro-attached vaginas! Varied views:
Wishful-thinking womanly well-hung wrecks!
Xanthodermic X-rated Xhosa 'X'!
Yard-enhancement! Yawning yonis! You!
Zygologists! Ziplessness! Zonkey zoo!

MECHANISM

Machines invariably work a change
Upon whatever they're designed to vary:
Position, motion, the human brain. Their compass
Is perfectly predictable, their lines
Functional. In creative writing circles
They're called 'poems'. You choose a word like 'lap'

And have to find six uses for it: lap.
Lap? The pen rebels! (You mustn't change
A key word once you've started.) The poem circles
Round and round like a vulture. If you vary
One single word, the vulture strikes. Your lines
Wobble like the needle of a compass.

What is the North you drive for with that compass?
What record are you breaking, lap after lap?
What walkabout could yield such sterile songlines?
What junction gives those lines a chance to change?
What signals stand at green and never vary?
What train of thought goes round in such small circles?

Yes, the sestina! Known in certain circles
As swinging sixes, its chosen words encompass
Something of your theme. *Change, vary,
Compass, lines, circles,* and finally *lap*
Are what you start with, and you simply change
Their order through the ensuing groups of lines.

They are hypnotic like an actor's lines
With which he charms the boxes, stalls and circles.
Or else they're like his face beneath each change
Of make-up, constant as a lover or a compass.
And some are like fast runners who outlap
The stragglers (last of all comes panting 'vary').

John Ashbery (a poet who likes to vary
His poem's drift at whim) says that its lines
Give him the feeling of sitting in the lap
Of a freewheeling cyclist spinning circles
Down the dizzy slope of sense, in its compass
All arbitrary meaning, wilful change.

But no. Its lines are quite controlled. They vary
Like petals in circles drawn by compasses
That six times overlap, and six times change.

PLEIADES

1 Alcyone
Daughter of Atlas, made an elder star,
Aloud asserts: 'To storm-led fleets a Phare!'

2 Electra
Door to a vatic gleam, Arcadian born,
You were the grief of Troy, and died each dawn.

3 Merope
Invisible as maiden, held to blame
For marrying a man, you died in shame.

4 Maia
'Hermes, my dear! – Heavens, I was a star
When Zeus came calling in his midnight car.'

5 Taygete
Nothing you did was greater than to die,
Allowed a certain future in the sky.

6 Celæno
You were the spirit-wind that night unlocks,
And, with all towns to storm, led fleets to rocks.

7 Asterope
Like hair of the Medusa, tutelar
Of human cities, best seen from afar.

LAUREL-CROWNED DECEPTIONS

'And what about your teachers who repeated: ars longa, vita brevis?
Their laurel-crowned deceptions will soon be over.
Do you still say to yourself: non omnis moriar?
O yes, not all of me shall die, there will remain
An item in the fourteenth volume of an encyclopædia
Next to a hundred Millers and Mickey Mouse.' Czeslaw Milosz

Czeslaw, you have a point. To be so famous
Must breed anxiety and much fatigue.
Not knowing you defines the ignoramus.
You are the striker of the superleague:
Czeslaw and Derek! Ted! Thom, Les and Seamus!
Fagged from a lifetime of sublime intrigue,
As confident as apple-pie in Eden,
Waiting for that telegram from Sweden.

But what will happen when you've won the prizes
And no one else is mentioned in the media?
It's true that reputation magnetises,
But there's a point when no one can get greedier.
The search for something that immortalises
Ends, after all, in that encyclopædia,
And even death can hardly seem too solemn
As long as you can claim at least a column.

Then there's Parnassus. Limelight never ceases!
A keen angelic audience awaits
A poet's very latest masterpieces
(Golden and clockwork twitterings from Yeats;
From Wordsworth, prosiness and anamnesis)
But, Czeslaw, pause before those pearly gates:
St Peter keeps two keys. The first is God's key.
The second (help!) belongs to Joseph Brodsky.

Of more recent poets, the ones who cut most dash
Are Philip Lark, Seams Heady and Silver Plash.
Lark originally belonged to something called The Movement,
Along with Kingly Aims and Win, but later showed some
    improvement.
Seams Heady, of course, is by no means the only
Irish poet. There is Paul Mullion, and even Michael Lonely.
If the life and works of Plash may seem a trifle rash,
She did owe a good deal to the confessional mode
Of the mad American poet Robert Lowed.

Donald Dave was in The Movement, too, but got more and more
Involved with Michael Stemmed, and became a bore
(This was a period when a majority of poets taught).
Lark had little influence, except on Anthony Thwart.
The gay Gnu was the best young poet of that decade, of
Course, but when Plash came he went – an unfortunate trade-off.
But then we have suffered such American swindles before,
As when we lost the great Western Aden. It seemed a kind of cheat
To be told that, well, we *had* after all gained T. S. Elite.

(American Poetry doesn't begin properly until Op,
But once it begins it really doesn't stop.
They are either large-gestured like Walleye Stevens or Sandbag
Or baroque and miscellaneous like Marine More's handbag.
There are formalists like Wilier or Tattoo
And wild men like Ed Drone or Gregory Coors who
Avoid the pentameter and go hippety-hop.
There is forbidding earnestness in poets like Oslo and Cruelly
And a compensating playfulness in, say, Gnash and Merrily.)

If you continue to press the right keys you will get more and more,
For poetry is like that (unless you re-try, abort, ignore).

A TOAST TO JAMES FENTON ON HIS
RELINQUISHMENT OF THE CHAIR OF POETRY

James Fenton, you've done it! You stood in the bread-line
(Or cake-line) and cut it and wished, and the deadline
Is met, the cake ate: and your term is completed,
You've managed to show off your cake and to eat it,
You've filled up your punnet,   James Fenton. You've done it!
The five years are over, you stand undefeated,
But ever since Fourth Week you've been quite unseated.

Is it really so long since your readers ensnared you
And the voters compared, and the Proctors declared you?
Is it really five years since we cheerfully Chaired you?
          Yes, we're here to see off   The quinquennial Prof,
The usual excuse for a swill and a scoff.
But look what occurred when you quietly retreated:
The Irish are back, and you can't say they cheated.

          Tom told us to fall in   And now we've brought Paul in,
And it's Hertford the new Prof will keep straw and stall in.
          The punning Muldoon   Will croon us a rune
On an Iroquois pipe to a leprechaun tune.
Elbows together, we've rigged the tarpaulin
And caulked us a vessel to weather a squall in.
Skipper, it's time for the change: you look all-in!
Auden referred to it thus: 'the Siege Perilous'.
But woe: there's no contest! Convocation is querulous
And the curates of Swindon go unbribed and sherryless.
          Is it really five years?   We can't credit our ears.
Astonishing, really, how time disappears.

But look here, there's one thing we shouldn't ignore:
You go back some distance, beyond '94.
You belong to the College. You were here long before.
October 15th, '67, I'm sure,
That Sunday of First Week, just after four?
When you came into Hall and there by the door
Was a welcoming tutor with *esprit de corps*

And a large metal teapot uplifted to pour?
(I'd been here a year, but was still pretty raw.)

From the north sneered Warren with marvellous mouth;
Westward was Waynflete; while to the south,
Bent, like a granny with knitting, was Routh:
All those challenging portraits, with freshmen beneath!
Philip Shaw Latimer, Kevin Dunseath,
Unshakeable Wintle with sociable teeth.
Kilroy was there   And Cronin, four-square,
And towering Phil Gooden with sceptical stare.

     But you were the star   The cleverest by far,
A mop of dark hair and a crimson *foulard*,
     A cup in your hand   And everything planned
In your own Golden Journey to Samarkand.
You had long left John Keats in his Faeryland:
It was Auden on whom you would take your stand.
You thought that The Movement was achingly bland,
And accused Dylan Thomas of adoring a gland,
As we talked by the teapot of pleasures in hand
And of some that seemed slightly less nice, even grim,
Like a jaw with Tom Boase or the Milton Prelim
(You didn't like it and you didn't like him).

     So you changed on a whim   Went out on a limb
Yes, later you read PPP to keep trim.
You scoured P. F. Strawson. You were much in the swim.
You met up with Hitchens and turned into Jim.
Your poems got tougher than some I still own
     (One couplet alone   Because it's unknown
Might keep me, if auctioned, in Hospice de Beâune).

     I have a memorial   Of that first-week tutorial,
A puzzling phrase in my diary, authorial
Certainly, teasingly conspiratorial.
     Here's how it reads: 'Write Fenton (night-steeds)'
But what can that signify? Memory recedes
Like the runway, perhaps, when you take the wrong airline,
Like ullage in port or a fifty-year hairline.

There's no going back   You're on the wrong track.
Your luggage key's lost and you fail to unpack.
     'Write Fenton (night-steeds).' Out of many good deeds
Was it that one that sowed one of poetry's seeds?
And if so, what *was* it exactly it sowed?
Did it linger in mind as a classical mode
Of allusion, a way to write poems in code?
Or was it the form? That Nativity Ode
Whose metrical ghost in 'Jerusalem' haunts
Those readers of yours who read Milton, and taunts
Them with echoes of thunderous music remembered
From the Puritan poet once thumbed and dismembered
In a Michaelmas Term by a Magdalen Demy,
A Repton ex-choirboy who wanted to try
At least for a week to do more than get by?

     Your mind was acuter   Than John Wayne's six-shooter.
Mine was a dredger and yours a freebooter;
As well play blitz chess with the latest computer;
Your pen had the power to make Byron look neuter:
How *could* I have thought of myself as your tutor?
It was like giving Wordsworth a tour of the dales
Or showing Canova what carving entails.
It was like making Beethoven practise his scales.

     In the next thirty years   So many careers!
So *many* tapes breasted to *so* many cheers
As you challenged your heroes and outpaced your peers
And left all your serious rivals in tears.
You've worked for the back and the front of the paper.
You've out-Kennethed Tynan and out-Tapered Taper.
     In each magazine   You were *chef de cuisine.*
You've out-Wystaned Auden, you've out-Grahamed Greene.
In Oxford, you're Arnold. In New York you're Ruskin.
There can't be a subject you don't wear subfusc in.
     You will cry out 'Aux armes!'   And come to no harm
You've been Stephen Sondheim with twice as much charm.
You cultivate roses. You've run a prawn farm.
You alarmingly smile when you bowl over-arm.

Your way with a chequebook would worry a banker:
You've rescued whole families, been their sheet-anchor.
On top of a tank you will scribble a tanka.
You'd be Groucho not Bogart in the film *Casablanca*.

And as for the Chair,   'You were marvellous' there:
You came to the footlights and bowed in the glare.
You moved to your lectern as if to the block,
One eye on your gown-ends and one on the clock,
And you smiled and you nodded around, taking stock
Of your regular flock   And St Cross chock-a-block.
And you unclipped your pages like picking a lock
And eased yourself into the warmth of your lecture
A bit like a pulpit but more like a deckchair
Where you mused at your leisure with comic conjecture
On dear D. H. Lawrence and Sylvia Plath,
The ideologue and the sociopath,
On Wystan Hugh Auden, the hurt polymath,
Mad Lowell, and Moore, with her Gothic coiffure,
Elizabeth Bishop, the grand voyageur,
Lion-jawed Ted Hughes, on the trail of his spoor,
And Larkin, the lift-man of literature.
(These I remember. There must have been more.)

I know (do *you* know?)   You're numero uno.
Your poetry's fine as an aria by Gounod.
It's bold as St Beuno   And fertile as Juno,
Politically wise as Miguel Unamuno.
It packs the same punch as Professor Frank Bruno.

So it's thank you to Fenton, to Jacob and James,
To Fenthing and Jimbo and multiple names
Of a multiple man with a multiple mind
Who has been both Professor and Poet combined.
Now we have dined   And variously wined
And it's time for the glass to be raised and inclined
To the lip, and the tongue and the liquid aligned,
And a toast to be drunk to our guest. Be so kind . . .

DANCE

INVITATION TO THE DANCE

Time has no standing here.
Time is out of mind.
So let him rave outside
And beat his fists upon our domes
With other accidents of cloud
And let him wail aloud
For what he will never find.

The room is full. Madame recruits
The clicking of two heels: a castanet!
That gilded looking-glass conceals
A secret cupboard where
The waiters can repair
A spoon's eclipse or want of flutes
And sidelong at their ease
View the reflection there
Of closing of the lips on cigarette
Or fingered tom-tom on the glacière.

Attention to a loosened curl
Suspended near
An unfamiliar ear
Absorbs a sworded earl.
An invitation to the dance
Cancels all insignificance,
The monster oozing charm,
His face upon her face,
Her breast in his embrace,
Her arm upon his arm.

The thudding of the oak excites
The jellies of the buffet, makes
Toes wag the space in pumps
And fans beat faster.
Under the trembling lights
The crystal shakes,
Couples revolve, give little jumps,
Turning whichever way
To scamper in their play
Beneath the flaking plaster.

Time has no standing still.
Time has his clock to climb.
And so we chase him hard
Till night comes up with something like
The day, and frivolous feet
Admitting no defeat
Keep on and on and on,
Keeping together,
Knowing they must keep time.

THE DANCE

World-eager, the joint
Straightened to a point
(Solomon rose in stone)
And to the temple
Came the temptress
(O my dove, my columb).

Shoulders stretched
And nails far-fetched
(Solomon rose in robes)
She asked again
What will remain
(O my dove, my quotient).

Though night advances
Shall we dance?
(Solomon rose in wine)
And still she asked
All that had passed
(O my dove, my trouble).

Ankle turned out
Lets toes sprout
(Solomon rose in blood)
Arms flung wide
At elbows divide
(O my dove, my double).

Knuckles unwhiten
As hands untighten
(Solomon rose in bone)
Part in a fan,
Stretch to their span
(O my dove, my nature).

Neck unlocks
And the heart knocks
(Solomon rose in fire)

And the waist twists
And turning wrists
(O my dove, my fixture).

Nothing that she required
Appeared to tire him
(Solomon rose again)
The night was entire
In its dome of fire
(O my dove, my turtle).

World-full, the heart
Must play its part
(Solomon rose again)
Dancing the answers
Dancing the dance
(O my dove, O my dove).

THE ARMPIT WALTZ

He is here! At my chair!
Shall I dance? Do I dare?
Lieber Baron! Mein Herr!

He
Throws his
Gloves through the air,
Like a magician's
Doves to his chair,
Glass in the fireplace!
Swords are superfluous!
From the beginning
His partner spinning
Works up a heat, pom-pom,
Whirls you off your feet, pom-pom.

And his diamond front, debonair,
And his flying hair everywhere
And the powerful hand you clasp
Makes you want to gasp your last
And you turn about so fast
That you must, you must, you must!
Since you'll be dust, be dust, be dust.

Strong
Hands
Huge on her backbone,
Fingering that track down
Precipitous boulders,
Powdered white shoulders
And the chute of the waist.

Her
Polished
Heel moves
Like a little wheel, proves
That what she's feeling
Is like dancing on the ceiling.
Now the Baron's reeling:
Life is bitter-sweet, pom–pom,
Pinch her country seat, pom–pom,
And the down of her spine there
Like the dawn on the Rhine where
The Baron might be sailing
And Loreleis wailing.

Look
There at
Shoulder blades pumping and
Double-basses thumping, and
Necklaces bouncing, and
Furbelows flouncing.

The
Poised and
Gently lifted foot knows
Where it should be put, goes
On the floor just there, yes?
Spin the little heiress!
See her glowing armpit shine
Like a distant farmpit, nein?
A little whiff of midden, it's
Practically hidden, sits
Hugged beneath the shoulder,
Snug as a candleholder.
Glug–glug, I'd like to sniff it!
It is beatific!
The nose is blessed, pom–pom,
Nuzzling in its nest, pom–pom,
In his dream of the Armpit Waltz.

THE CAPTAIN'S GALOP

Quickly running sideways: such an idiotic thing to do,
Arms around the waists of sexual persons either side of you!

Portholes show the ocean lifting: when the deck begins to tilt
Dancing feet continue to express a faith in how it's built.

Locked together, silk to flannel, epaulette to mutton-sleeve,
Men and women not related boldly pair and interweave.

Hugged so closely, don't you feel the secret grinding of the hips,
Like a millipede proceeding drunkenly with little skips?

Might you care to flick an ankle? Squeeze a bottom? Laugh out
    loud?
Once the fiddlers start to sweat you'll find that little's disallowed.

Chin up high, and beaming, face the left as you approach the
    right,
Smartly turn the head to starboard, giving whoops of pure delight.

Always looking back to where you came from when you make
    the turn,
Measuring each distance with a merry air of unconcern.

Underneath you, ocean turning restlessly from side to side,
Salt illimitable litres mindlessly preoccupied.

Captain's table: dizzy still, the dancers turn to langoustines.
Silver ladles swirl like hands of clocks around the soup tureens.

Baudroie, merlan, grondin, vive, goggle up from bouillabaisse,
Challenging Lord Challenger to look them calmly in the face.

Mrs Thing attempts a pudding (ewe's cheese, sugar, eau-de-vie).
Angela's left knee beneath the table feels another knee.

Fruit and walnuts, laughs and murmurs, sweet phlogiston of cigars.
Captain's toast: the poised ecstatic metaphysics of the stars.

North to south and east to west unbroken line of night and sea,
Scattered in their milky dome the lights in vague immensity.

Named once for the legions of the heavens supervising earth,
Minting men and women with their life-long character at birth.

Glasses raised, the stars are praised in sips of port for all they teach,
Light fingers of applause, the tug of chairs, and now the Captain's
        speech:

'Whither bound, and why? The thumping questions tease as
        questions will,
Searching in the testaments for some revealing codicil.

God made everything there is, from cochineal to caribou.
God who made the boundless waters turned his hand to me and
        you.

Apemen, alemen, archers, abbots, applewomen, advocates,
Educators, engineers, eccentrics, excommunicates,

Introverts, inspectors, intellectuals, irrationalists,
Owners, overseers, officials, oboists, oenologists,

Unbelievers, utter bastards, underlings, utopians:
Each vocation has its blueprint somewhere in his doodled plans.

Ask me how I know this? I'm the Captain. I must know.
Pilot, vicar, host, philosopher and impresario.

Souls entrusted to my care and *nothing* ever left to chance,
Daily orders, perfect freedom, all you have to do is dance.

Don't you bless me for your pleasures? Don't you leap at my
        commands?
Know your destiny is safely locked away and in my hands?

Dance the dance in every calm and dance the dance through every
        storm.
Dance the headlong dance that dancing surely meant us to perform.

Keep the dancing line unbroken, dance together, never stop.
Dance the Captain's dance. The bouncing, hectic, thunderous Galop!'

THE FIGUE MAXIXE

Green outside and pink within,
Figs must be the fruit of sin.
Le long de l'Esplanade de Nice
Suck them and dance the Figue Maxixe:
Wearing a great big sticky grin,
D'abord on tord, et puis on glisse.
That's how to do the Max, Max,
That's how to do the Figue Maxixe.

Princesse de Polignac est protectrice,
Protège de génie et Des Six.
Elle donne le sein à son salon,
Et ô ses petits mamelons
Américains! They make you shiver.
So does the down upon her Swanee River.
That's where they learned the Max, Max,
That's where they learned the Figue Maxixe.

Elle est si raffinée. Elle est exquise.
Elle port les pyjama en raies cerises.
Princess of the sewing machine,
Elle donne de l'argent et de sa poitrine.
First one foot and then the other:
Who's the baby? Who's the mother?
She dotes upon the Max, Max,
Si raffolée du Figue Maxixe.

The Princess wears a cakewalk wig.
The Princess just adores a fig,
Petit sac avec semence:
Dans son douceur elle s'y enfonce.
Ses lèvres lestes se reconnaissent:
D'abord elles tordent et puis elles glissent
That's how she does the Max, Max,
That's how she does the Figue Maxixe.

Princesse de Polignac est très polie.
Princesse de Polignac n'est point poilue.
L'Enfer Blanc de Pitz-Palu
A fait son maquillage pâli.
Princess de Polignac est ma délice,
And most of all I like her knees,
So let's all do the Max, Max,
Let's all do the Figue Maxixe.

THE ORBITAL SAMBA

The lights on the shore and the crowds as they roar and the
    rhythm are leading you townwards
And the drums as they beat get into your feet like the rum
    when the bottle tilts downwards
And it runs through the veins where it plans its campaigns
    like Wellesley before Salamanca.
Your arms are in bud with splayed fingers and blood; each
    side-kick you give is a spanker.
One hip like a rocket departs from its socket while the other
    revolves on its axis
And the whole body sways as the pelvis sashays and the
    spine absolutely relaxes.
You decide that it's pleasant to feel deliquescent and notice
    that people around you
With their arms in the air and with glittering hair are edging
    their way to surround you,
For you are the star that they sense from afar like matter
    obedient to gravity,
The luminous centre they all wish to enter, the focus of total
    depravity.
Your limbs are balletic, your skin is magnetic, your gaze is
    compelling as granite,
Your merest inaction's a fatal attraction, the force that sets
    spinning the planet.
No wonder the dance is biology's chance to shuffle its cards
    for the future:
Not only the samba but also the mambo, the maypole, the
    Minnie-the-Moocher,
The Palais at Harlesden, the can-can, the Charleston, the
    knees-up, the Countess of Cavan,
The one-in-a-million, the twist, the cotillion, the polka, the
    brawl and the pavane,
The Highlander's sword-dance, the fling, the Gay Gordons,
    the Iroquois war-dance, the goose-step,
The Argentine tango, the reel, the fandango, the clog-dance,
    the one-step, the two-step.

You're surrounded by persons whose self-control worsens as
their hair falls to pieces when the tempo increases (in
the greeny-brown light it's Pre-Raphaelite, all bouncing
and frizzy: think Rossetti and Lizzy) and you can't get
away from the flashing array of criss-crossing lasers and
stoned star-gazers; the infant heart-breakers and
quivering Quakers and ecstasy-fakers; the mischief-
makers, tattooed undertakers and lewd Sabbath-
breakers; the amateur Shakers and Josephine Bakers: it's
enough to send you bananas.

THE QUAQUAVERSAL JIG

Left, right, feeling your own sides,
Smoothing down the waist.
     Your hips jut
As you level the ground about you
     With concentration.
     Left. Right.
Such pow-wow tells the body
It has become the god it worships.
     Your eyes are shut
     In self-admiration.

Left, right, brushing the cobwebs away,
Peering through the weight of the music.
     A duck and a hunch,
Cocking the head on the shoulders,
     Stomping on the spot.
     Left. Right.
Such sense of body needs no witness,
No agreement to touch, no devotion.
     Thanks a lot.
     Thanks a bunch.

THE FINAL DANCE

Motion, we thought, was purely our will
To be at once in different places,
As though there were such places to fill
From which we drew the energy
To prosecute our endless pleasures.
Not just the shadows that others cast,
Like enough in shape to our own,
But rare uninhabited spaces
That lit up when we entered them.
We could not bear to be alone.
And so we danced, a tousled romp
That knew in its heart it could not last,
Dance after dance, a reckless drill,
Dance after dance, a frenzy of gesture,
The marathon stare, the glad-handed stomp.
Whatever we did, it was open to question,
Timed to the close, to the thrill, to the dare,
Done for itself, and with nobody there.
The final dance of all is keeping still.

ACKNOWLEDGEMENTS AND NOTES

Many of the poems were written to themes and forms set by the Secretary of the John Florio Society of Magdalen College, and first aired there. I would like to dedicate the whole collection to past and present members of the Society. Grateful acknowledgement is also made to the following publications, in which some of these poems first appeared: *Agenda, Areté, Kadmos, Magdalen College Record, Oxford Magazine, Oxford Poetry, Poetry Nation Review, Poetry Review* and the *Times Literary Supplement*.

'Never Knew' is written to the tune of 'Hector', by J. Manse and C. Oberfield, as recorded by Fernandel in 1940.

'The Curse of the Glass Back Lanky Coolie': the eponymous complainant is a fireman on the Lancashire and Yorkshire Railway who isn't keen on heavy work. 'Clear pop': no stopping signals recorded. 'Feathers': direction signals. 'Pounded': shunted to a siding. 'Dark time': money for night work. 'Lemonjolly': melancholy. 'Blue Streak': Midland Pullman. 'Bowling Green': fast line. 'Long Tom': large coals. 'Nozzle': nose. 'Navvies' wedding cake': bread pudding. 'Fireplaces': false teeth. 'Jumping jacks': inquisitive foremen. 'Snapscran': sandwich tin.

'The Only Got So Much Blues' was written for *Seven Deadly Sins*, ENO's private farewell to Mark Elder, Peter Jonas, David Pountney and Edmund Tracey at the Great Hall, Lincoln's Inn, on 13 June 1993, with music by Robin Holloway.

In 'The Spellchecker's Guide to Poetry' all the names were the automatic and helpful corrections of Microsoft's Word 6.1.

In 'At a Distance', *prut in pure* is the bride in the bower, and the joke about strong views is borrowed from A. J. P. Taylor.

The autogram is, so far as I know, a new form of poetic biography: the imitation of the poet's work is limited to using only the letters found in his or her name.

'The Poet Orders his Marriage at St Marylebone Church' was commissioned by the Browning Society and Poet in the City to commemorate the marriage of Robert and Elizabeth Barrett Browning on the 160th anniversary of that occasion on 12 September 2006.

'A Toast to James Fenton' was proposed in Common Room after dinner at Magdalen College on 3 June 1999.

73